A Poetic Odyssey of Proclamations

May'24

Dear Benjamin,

So much lies ahead of you
Seize every golden opportunity
to grow and have an impact.
Your "stage" awaits you.

[illegible] x

A Poetic Odyssey of Proclamations

*31 ways to sow,
grow and flow
goodness into
your life*

Peju Abuchi

A Poetic Odyssey of Proclamations
31 ways to sow, grow and flow goodness into your life

ISBN 9781739807214

Published by CORE Leaders International Publishing.

Peju Abuchi
www.pejuabuchi.com

Cover design and interior design: Hester van Toorenburg
www.naiabookdesign.com

It takes a community to write a book so I am forever grateful to the pillars of strength that surround me. My husband, Obi, for how much he has championed my vision of birthing this first book. Thank you for being the empowering wind beneath my wings. Our three boys will always be my joy and crown, no matter how tall and strong they become. Thank you, Hester, for your patience and positivity in bringing this beautiful book to life. Last, but not least, to all the women and men who have seen and relentlessly called out greatness from within me - Thank you.

I Am because You Are!

Praise For A Poetic Odyssey of Proclamations

"Peju's latest offering is not just a book; it is an invitation to engage with the world—and with oneself—in a more meaningful way. Through her compelling mix of poetry, focus questions, and personal proclamations, she has created a unique resource that has the power to change lives. This book is more than just a good read; it's a roadmap to a better, more fulfilling existence."

***Caroline Ribeiro-Nelson**, Founder & Head of Free Choices, Diverse Mental Health*

"As gentle rainfall makes the desert bloom, so Peju's words sprinkle their truth on a stony world. This book, in its honesty and sincerity, awakens in the hearts of all who read it a flowering of humility, wisdom and kindness."

***Alastair Graham**, Principal, Hall Grove School*

"This is a beautiful piece of work I can see myself coming back to over and over again, either as a daily meditation, or as the various topics it touches upon are more relevant to my situation. I highly recommend this to anyone who doesn't want to just go with the flow that negative circumstances in your life may be suggesting you have to. You can use this to grow through it, and take charge for you, those around you, and the world at large."

***Maxine Nwaneri,** Bestselling Author & Founder of The Future is Greater*

"This book is rich in creative responses to the challenges and phases of life. Taking one of the thirty-one "Proclamations" each day for a month could lift a person's life as they "Pause and Ponder" on their own situation."

Mark Moody-Stuart, *Former Vice Chair of the UN Global Compact and former Chair of the Global Compact Foundation*

"I love the way that Peju encourages all of us to find our inner wordsmith by writing our own proclamations, inspired by hers. This book is truly life affirming and has rejuvenated my curiosity in myself, my emotions and my relationships with the world and those around me."

Angela Davies, *Coach and Healthcare Leader*

"My favourite proclamation is "In your sadness, proclaim community." The author addresses the universal experience of sadness and emphasizes the significance of having a supportive network of friends and family during challenging times. This proclamation underscores the importance of reaching out and nurturing relationships, reminding us that we are not alone in our struggles. This book is precious."

Simona Barbieri, *HubDot Founder & Creative Director*

"A Poetic Odyssey of Proclamations is a masterfully curated masterpiece. It cleverly blends poetry with philosophy, inspiration with realism, and draws the reader into a deeper place where they can pause, soul search and reflect. The book simultaneously encourages, challenges, soothes and inspires."

Bola Ogundeji, *People Director, London Legacy Development Corporation*

"I help diverse corporate women to have better mental health and this powerful book of proclamations is a poetic masterpiece to empower women who are tired of fighting oppression. Your words will speak life into the Kinship community."

Marteka Swaby, *Coach & Founder, Benevolent Health*

"Peju delivered a powerful compilation of daily affirmations. Her book is a thoughtful and practical guide designed to help almost anyone unleash their potential, one step at a time."

Lau Ciocan, *TEDx Speaker and Founder of Mentoring Advocacy Network (MAN)*

"A powerful book for living, packed with humour, vulnerability and wisdom. A brilliant debut."

Aduke Onafowokan, *Founder, The Sister Sister Network*

"This book weaves together inspiration with firm but gentle nudges that invite the reader to participate and experience a revolutionary change! I love It!"

Anyima Quarm Okundi, *Executive Coach & Reflective Partner for Inner Landscape Change Work*

"This is an outstanding, practical companion to life in our digitally interactive twenty-first century, with encouraging words relevant to a human of any age. Peju's friendly and richly compassionate understanding of our varied everyday states of mind encourage the reader to take action."

Judy Moody-Stuart, *longterm supporter of The Asian University for Women, Bangladesh*

"Peju Abuchi's poetic odyssey is a wonderful, uplifting gift, reflecting her own poetic gift. In a world of so much anxiety and despair, this book is relentlessly positive and refreshingly hopeful. I particularly appreciated the simple 'Pause' exercises accompanying each theme."

Pete Greig, *Senior Pastor, Emmaus Rd Church and Founder, 24-7 Prayer International*

"Read this book and then reread it. Take your time, speed up, read it selectively, read it collectively, read it in sequence and then out of sequence. For all of life's moments and for any life moment, Peju's guidance and wisdom helps you to navigate the contours of this "curvy" life journey as well as provide the space to lean into your own affirming power and words."

Dr Doyin Atewologun, *Business Psychologist and Executive Leadership Coach, Founder, Delta Alpha Psi*

"What a gift for young and old alike; for all sorts, for everyone who seeks to be blessed and in turn be a blessing, for each person who will take the time to bask in the simple beauty of each day's call. Every single one of them brought a sense of unrelenting hope and felt like fuel for my soul. I love that there are words from the author to deeply inspire, space for our own intimate and raw reflections and a page for our own personal proclamations. I proclaim that this book will change the lives of the many who will receive and read it!

'Ronke Kokoruwe, *Founder, iVerbalize (and a very proud sister)*

Dedication

This first book of mine is dedicated to my wonderful parents - Prince Adegoke and Olori Ayodipupo Ademiluyi. You have been my most vocal fans, my most loyal cheerleaders and a fountain of blessing in my life that never runs dry. You consistently speak words of blessing, beauty and brilliance over me and into me - I am forever grateful for you and your legacy of goodness to me.

'Peju

Contents

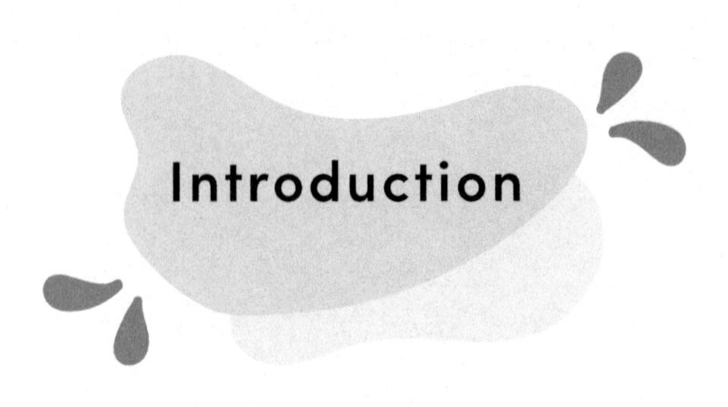

Introduction

The sayings – "You build your world with your words" and "Your words make up your world" - reverberate over the centuries and are just as true in this day and age as they were in ancient times. Young and old alike now have access to so much information, having been thrust into the eye of the social media storm, rife with words upon words.

Words are powerful! There is power in the spoken word! There is also power in the words we tell ourselves that form the foundational beliefs that we live by.

Proclamations, affirmations and declarations invite us all on a new journey – to take charge and speak life, love and limitless opportunities into ourselves, our close and distant communities and our world at large.

An odyssey is described in The Britannica Dictionary as *"A long journey full of adventures; a series of experiences that give knowledge or understanding to someone."*

In this poetic odyssey, you will learn to choose your words carefully, use your words strategically and attract goodness rhythmically to firstly, build a world that you want to live in, and then to ignite that same world with powerfully, potent, poetic proclamations.

How to get the most out of this book

These proclamations can be used again and again, for yourself or on behalf of others – in every season of life. Proclamations work with practice.

Use them in your personal daily meditation.
Use them with a trusted circle of friends and share your musings with courage and compassion.

This odyssey gives you many opportunities to pause and ponder by asking you to dig deeper with questions relating to each proclamation and by giving you the chance to deepen your understanding by writing your own personal proclamations. Have fun with this. Your words are powerful! Allow your innermost thoughts to flow as you seek to grow and glow.

- Part 1 -

For the emotions that come with being alive

Having emotions is a sign that we are human. Emotions help us communicate with others and they also help us check in with ourselves. They help us put language to our humanity. But, they are just that - emotions.

They may give us ways of understanding ourselves and others, but, they need not lead us nor master us. We are responsible for what we do with our emotions and how we navigate the landscape of life with them.

Gratitude

I know gratitude
Is a great attitude
So, I will proclaim it loudly!
And count my blessings proudly

- 1 -

In your life, proclaim gratitude

Gratitude is one of those arenas you can't tire of being in. It is an absolute game-changer and as long as there is breath in your lungs and your heart is beating, you have a million and more things to be grateful for. Gratitude makes most things look better, feel better, taste better and sound better. Let all of your life reverberate with gratitude.

Pause & Ponder

What five things are you most grateful for today?

Proclamations

Write your personal **Gratitude** proclamation

Praise

I proclaim that in my pain
There is still so much to gain
So, I'll change my frame
And bless this game

- 2-

In your pain, proclaim praise

No one likes to feel pain or sit with pain. It can be uncomfortable, unrelenting and downright unjust! How bizarre – at a time when you feel most vulnerable, your biggest need could be to shout out in praise everything that is still worthy of being called a blessing in your life.

Could praise become an antidote to your pain?

Pause & Ponder

Where is your greatest pain point right now?

Proclamations

Write your personal **Praise** proclamation

Hope

Joy and hope go hand in hand
They play the loudest music in the band!
So, I will radiate my joy
It leaves others wanting more and more

- 3-

In your joy, proclaim hope

It feels so good to feel so good. Joy is contagious in that it waters every part of your body and then overflows like a fresh spring to shower and nurture others around you. Joy has the power of magnetism – do not downplay it! It gives hope to others of a brighter tomorrow.

Pause & Ponder

How can your joy give hope to someone this week?

Proclamations

Write your personal **Hope** proclamation

Courage

The shadows may feel comfortable
But steeped in them I'm not able
To courageously step into the light
And proclaim that my life is a delight!

- 4 -

In the shadows, proclaim courage

The "shadows" can feel like that unsettling mid-point between light and darkness. You're not quite in the dark but neither do you want to step fully into the light of your life. Proclaim courage in this season – sometimes that means putting one foot in front of the other and facing the light at the tunnel's end.

Pause & Ponder

What does stepping out in courage look like today?

Proclamations

Write your personal **Courage** proclamation

Wisdom

I proclaim that in this darkness I am growing
I am gathering seeds and sowing
I may be weeping
But in wisdom, I am also reaping!

- 5-

In your dark times, proclaim wisdom

Dark times are not all bad. Think of all the growth that happens in the dark – the roots of trees get embedded deeply into the soil and start an intricate communication network with other roots; in the deep dark of night, as you sleep, your body and mind receive vital nourishment, rejuvenation and a chance to reset. Don't despise your dark times, in them proclaim wisdom!

Pause & Ponder

What two ways can you grow through
the dark times you're currently in?

Proclamations

Write your personal **Wisdom** proclamation

Clarity

My confusion is lifting
And NOW clarity is gifting-
me with the vision that I need
For the signs that I read

- 6-

In the confusion, proclaim clarity

In our fast-paced, forward-facing and multi-faceted world, it is so easy to be confused. There is a plethora of choice – from toothpastes to car insurance policies, from lipstick shades to holiday package deals and from herbal tea flavours to politicians who take "favours." We are quick to second guess our decisions when social media influencers don't back us up. We have become wary and weary of making mistakes. Our confusion rises like smoke from an industrial chimney. Proclaim clarity!

Pause & Ponder

In which three areas of life do you need clarity right now?

Proclamations

Write your personal **Clarity** proclamation

Equality

The Goodness Pie is large enough for all
So, I will answer the call
To make way for another
And not see them as a bother.

- 7-

In your plenty, proclaim equality

What a wonderful feeling to be in a season of life where you are experiencing abundance. An abundance of goodness is what we all desire – good times, good friends, good food, good standard of living – the good life! Yet, you can easily get caught up in your abundance that you forget the multitude who are crying out for a piece, or perhaps a crumb, of that same Goodness Pie. Remember, equality will not diminish your plenty; on the contrary, it promises to enrich the plenty.

Pause & Ponder

Who are you aware of who needs support to access some of the Goodness Pie?

Proclamations

Write your personal **Equality** proclamation

Community

Depression may surround my flesh and bones
But in my sadness, I am not alone
I am encircled by loving family and friends
With them I will navigate all my uncanny bends

-8-

In your sadness, proclaim community

Sadness is real and sad times come to us all. However, the most challenging part of experiencing a sad season is the feeling of loneliness and isolation that ruthlessly comes alongside our feelings of doom and despair. A trustworthy circle of friends and family is key at this time – they are your support system and play a huge part in your journey to recovery. It takes a village to raise a child and it takes a community to nurture an adult.

Pause & Ponder

Who is in your community and whose community are you in?

Proclamations

Write your personal **Community** proclamation

Triumph

The movie of my life is a very depressing drama
Trauma surrounds me like a ring of fire
But, I will triumph, I will grow higher and higher
The victory that is coming,
this present mourning can't decipher!

- 9-

In your trauma, proclaim triumph

Sometimes, life feels like a house of thorns – as though trauma has chosen specifically to live with you. And trauma, like a silent death sentence, leaves you terrified and paralysed. Its effects spill over into every area of your life. This is the season to proclaim triumph from your trauma – to know you can grow from it and become victorious! This is the power of post-traumatic growth.

Pause & Ponder

What does post-traumatic growth look like to you in this season?

Proclamations

Write your personal **Triumph** proclamation

Boldness

This grief will not define me
This is my most urgent plea
I will face the pain, I will not flee
Through it all, I am becoming more of who
I want to be

-10-

In the fragility of life, proclaim boldness

Different things happen in life which can sneak up on you and steal your confidence – a car accident, a failed exam, a divorce, the death of a significant person, the loss of valuable friendships, weight gain, feeling undervalued and discontented at work, family discord, unfulfilled dreams, financial frustrations and so forth. You could end up feeling fragile and small. Time to proclaim boldness! Not denial or cockiness, but genuine boldness.

Pause & Ponder

What has stolen your confidence?

Proclamations

Write your personal **Boldness** proclamation

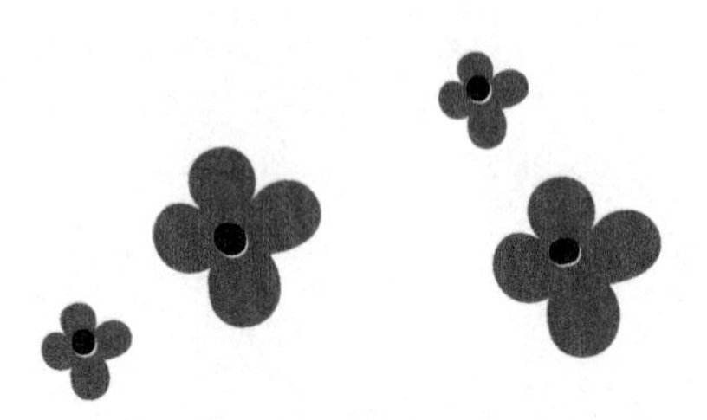

Peace

I proclaim peace over my mind, body and soul
Blossoming through boundary-setting is now my goal
I am present, I am full of purpose and I am whole
Going forward, I relinquish the pressure to always be in control

- 11 -

In your exhaustion, proclaim peace

Do you feel tired and restless? Unable to get through your daily list of must-dos and have-tos and to-dos? Welcome to the human race. Even with the voracious advancement of technology, human beings are more tired than ever through the increasing pressure of doing everything, being everywhere and knowing everyone. FOMO (Fear Of Missing Out) has become the coveted state of being. How exhausting!

Pause & Ponder

Where do you need to set the biggest boundaries
to protect your inner peace?

Proclamations

Write your personal **Peace** proclamation

JOMO

It may appear that I'm missing out
But only for the things I need not worry about
In the most important areas, my joy is increasing
I stand in awe as I see my fear decreasing

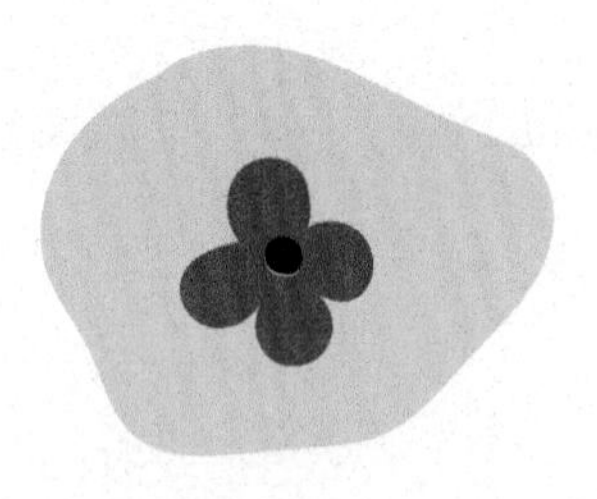

- 12-

In your FOMO, proclaim JOMO

The truth is, you can't be everywhere, all the time, doing everything, with everyone. Something's got to give and so often, you sacrifice your mental health and self-care to try to please everyone. That is, until you realise how miserable and unfulfilled you are! Taper your FOMO (Fear Of Missing Out) with JOMO (Joy Of Missing Out). You will experience a joy and ease that helps you to grow and glow, without the constant need to compare yourself to others.

Pause & Ponder

What are 3 benefits of letting go of
the constant fear of missing out?

Proclamations

Write your personal **JOMO** proclamation

Rest

I can only be at my best when I fully rest
Otherwise, everything seems like a very hard test
I invite solace to be my daily guest
A life seasoned with laughter is now my choice of zest

- 13-

In your times of stress, proclaim rest

Stress seems to be a constant life partner. An increasing number of us are feeling the pinch and punch of mental health ailments and it is affecting the quality of your lives, your effectiveness at work, the joy in your relationships and your hope for the future. Some of you are so under-rested, you have become aliens to what constitutes relaxation and fun. Remember, life's simple pleasures still ease stress and centre us. Choose a few to engage in and...breathe.

Pause & Ponder

Which three simple pleasures will you indulge in this week?

Proclamations

Write your personal **Rest** proclamation

Abundance

Hard times come and go
And through them abundance can flow
Right now, I may be feeling low
But I trust that my field of greatness will grow

- 14-

In your hard times, proclaim abundance

"Times are hard!" we repeat over and over again and then, guess what? Times just continue to feel hard! We need to watch our words and speak abundance into our hard times. Every cloud does have a silver lining and every dark night does break forth into the light of a new day!

So many people, like you and me, have used their tough times to build resilience, become successful and shine the light for others to follow. You can become another testimony to this. Join the club!

Pause & Ponder

How can you grow this week from a scarcity mindset to an abundance mindset?

Proclamations

Write your personal **Abundance** proclamation

Joy

My heart will heal
It may take time
Deep joy I can feel
In the midst of this grime

- 15-

In your heartache, proclaim joy

Is it possible to find joy in pain? Is it possible to laugh with a broken heart? Can healing come while you're aching? When you focus on the heartache, it feels BIGGER than you – an insurmountable mountain that you can never overcome. But, when your gaze moves to someone, somewhere or something that uplifts you, the ache feels less like a mountain and more like a steep hill that you can get over – in time.

Pause & Ponder

What can bring you joy today while your heart is aching?

Proclamations

Write your personal **Joy** proclamation

Freedom

This storm will not devour me
Though the pain stings like a vicious bee
I will learn what I must, I will not flee
Freedom is on my horizon, it's a calm and peaceful sea

- 16-

In your storms, proclaim freedom

At any given season, you will be sailing on different seas to those around you. What is the "sea" like in this season of your life? Is there a tempest in your sea or are you surfing on the waves of peace? Nobody wants to remain in a storm, especially when you feel like you're right in the middle of it – the dreaded "eye of the storm." Choose to proclaim freedom from the ravages of the storm so that you can embrace the pain, lean in and learn from it.

Pause & Ponder

How can you become more of a student of the storm you are currently in?

Proclamations

Write your personal **Freedom** proclamation

Restoration

My regrets are a shallow grave
They keep me imprisoned in this crazy maze
Restoration is what I deeply crave
So, I will move forward, precious relationships to save

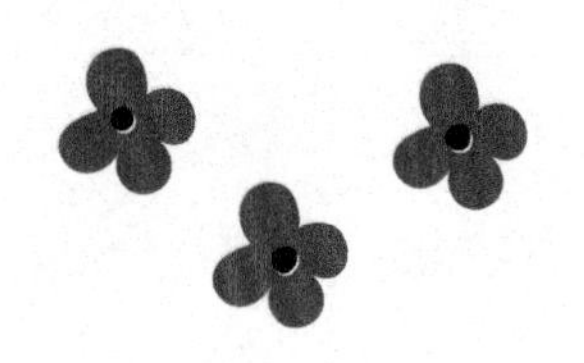

- 17-

In your regrets, proclaim restoration

"Regret" seems like such a taboo word. You wish you could sail through life and look back on a flawless record of perfection. Fortunately, that is not how life works. As long as you are alive, you will continue to make mistakes. It is part of the brokenness and humility of being human.

Some of your biggest regrets are centred around broken or lost relationships. You regret what you've said, who you've said it to, how you said it or where you were when you said it. The list goes on and on...

It is impossible to "unsay" what you've said or to "undo" what you've done, but it is possible to proclaim restoration in this season – an opportunity to redeem the situation and the relationship - and watch good grow from it.

Pause & Ponder

How can you begin to restore a broken relationship this week?

Proclamations

Write your personal **Restoration** proclamation

Calm

My inner voice softly speaks-

calm into my anxious weeks

And though my anxiety I can't fix

Calm fills me up, out chaos leaks

- *18*-

In your anxiety, proclaim calm

"Calm down!" has been noted as one of the most unhelpful things to say to someone feeling anxious or responding to a crisis. It just seems to heighten the anxiety. Yet, personally proclaiming calmness in your seasons of anxiety, stress and frustration may be very helpful. If you can trust your inner voice, speaking calm over yourself and into your mind and soul won't seem intrusive but very intuitive.

Pause & Ponder

How can calmness become your ally in anxious times?

Proclamations

Write your personal **Calm** proclamation

Forgiveness

Now, we are clearly divided
But with forgiveness we can be united
I now set myself free
By offering forgiveness when we disagree

- 19 -

In your discord, proclaim forgiveness

One of the most challenging arenas of life is disagreement and discord, especially with family and friends. If someone cuts ahead of you in a shopping queue or on the road while you're driving, you may feel slighted for a few minutes. However, you move on and choose not to waste too much energy on a stranger.

On the other hand, an awful misunderstanding or disagreement with the ones you love or care about can hurt very deeply and take years to reconcile. It is so much harder to move on.

The answer?

Forgiveness – firstly, for yourself and then for the other. It's been said that forgiveness can heal a lot of mess. It sets us free so we can see clearly what step to take next.

Pause & Ponder

Who do you need to set free by forgiving?

Proclamations

Write your personal **Forgiveness** proclamation

Opportunity

Opportunity knocks in my desperation
I will not answer with trepidation
Now, the consideration of my decision
Will be for choices that lead to celebration

- 20-

In your desperation, proclaim opportunity

Sometimes, it feels like you're carrying the weight of the world on your shoulders and the pressure is weighing you down, big time! Desperate times call for desperate measures, or do they? Humans have been known to make the worst decisions in their desperation. You feel pressured on all sides and that clouds your judgement. You then look back and feel regret and shame for how low you stooped because of how desperate you were. This is a season to proclaim opportunity out of your desperation.

Pause & Ponder

Where are the opportunities arising out of your desperation?

Proclamations

Write your personal **Opportunity** proclamation

Self-love

How do I love me?
Let me count the ways –
Not only on good days
When I feel the sun's rays

I long to gaze
At my current phase
And express self-love with a
powerful phrase –
"I am a beautiful blaze!"

This is my current craze
As I navigate life's maze
Watch me dazzle and daze
I will amaze!

My glorious reflection says
That I love me in all ways
Till the end of my days
Even as my hair glows with greys!

- 21-

In your shame, proclaim self-love

Shame – that accusatory feeling that points the finger and tells you how bad you are. It shouts down at you to think mean and nasty thoughts about how you look, what you've done, what you're thinking and what you've said. Shame is not an ally. Shame is not a friend. Shame does not provide good counsel.

When shame rears its very ugly head, proclaim the power of self-love! Choose not to define yourself by your deeds, however shocking they may be. You can change. You are bruised and broken, but there is still beauty buried within you. Nurture it and it will grow.

Self-acceptance and self-love are the foundation for healthy living and the solid bricks for building healthy relationships.
It starts with you.

Hence, a longer and deeper proclamation is included here. Own it and proclaim it!

Pause & Ponder

What five things do you cherish about yourself?

Proclamations

Write your personal **Self-love** proclamation

Direction

My fears are not my master
Instead, I choose to muster-
the little strength that I have to foster-
Trust, as divine direction leads me away from disaster

- 22-

In your fear, proclaim direction

What are you afraid of? Really, what scares the living daylights out of you? It could be anything from spiders to clowns, from public speaking to rejection, from loneliness to death. Your fears are real. They may not make sense to the next person but they are a huge part of what governs your reality. Having said that, your fears need not control you or you will become their servant – answering to their every whim and whistle.

On the flip side, your fears can act as useful guides – alarm bells that can alert you to danger. This is where they work with you, not against you. Proclaiming direction in this tricky season will support you in moving forward and leading your fears, not following them.

Pause & Ponder

In what way can your current fears act as allies, not adversaries?

Proclamations

Write your personal **Direction** proclamation

Self-compassion

I may feel broken time and time again
Yet empathy tells me I am not insane
So, I will lavish myself with space and grace
To enjoy running my own unique race

- *23*-

In your brokenness, proclaim self-compassion

How easy it is to beat yourself up when you're down, when you falter and fail or when others call you worthless. The most valuable journey for each individual is on the road to self-compassion and self-acceptance. So, when next you fall, gently pick yourself up and wrap arms of understanding and empathy around yourself. It will work wonders!

Pause & Ponder

What does empathy towards yourself look like?

Proclamations

Write your personal **Empathy** proclamation

- Part 2 -

For the phases in your life

There are some life phases that connect us all – childhood, ageing, education, work and marriage. They are not emotions in and of themselves but they definitely evoke a myriad of feelings and sensations that you need to face head-on or sometimes, just sit with.

Acceptance

Ageing well is on my bucket list
I want to enjoy it as a much-anticipated feast
And if life throws my way shadows in the midst of it,
I will choose to accept, not resentfully resist

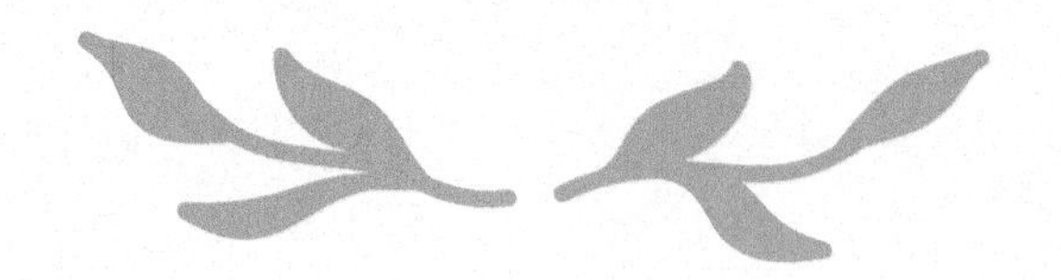

- 24-

In your ageing, proclaim acceptance

Growing old can be compared to a cloak we all want to wear, at the right time. A cloak that isn't too heavy, scratchy or ill-fitting but one that is colourful, cashmere to touch and inviting.

Ageing is a blessing and although it is rife with its own challenges, you can make good choices now that will impact how comfortable the cloak of old age will be later. One of the most important ways to approach getting old, whether in yourself or in your loved ones, is through the power of acceptance. Take responsibility and do your best to stay mentally fit, physically healthy and all-round positive, now.

The overall process of ageing is a part of life. Choose to accept that and lean into it with humour and honour.

Pause & Ponder

In what ways can you see growing old as a blessing?

Proclamations

Write your personal **Acceptance** proclamation

Happiness

Your childhood is a time for so much good
To enter your heart and nurture you with soul-food
I proclaim happiness over your young days
May you feel the warmth and glow
of the brightest sun rays

- 25-

In their childhood, proclaim happiness

Oh, the joys of being a child – the time in your life when you have full permission to be silly, spontaneous and sweet. Childhood should be synonymous with laughter, giggling and goofing around. But we know that sadly, this isn't the case for millions of children in the world. Life grows them up too quickly and they experience far too much trauma for their young hearts and minds.

One of the nicest ways to grow up is to look back on heaps of happy memories of your childhood. That joy truly lifts you up on your sad adult days and puts a sparkle in your eyes as you look to the future.
Proclaim happiness over every child you know – its collective energy will flow around the world and spread good cheer!

Pause & Ponder

How can you bring happiness to a child's life this week?

Proclamations

Write your personal **Happiness** proclamation

Guidance

I am surrounded by adults I can trust
And although I don't do everything they say I must
I know they want the best for me
Their guidance really helps me "see"

- 26-

In your teenage years, proclaim guidance

The teenage years – filled with so much self-discovery, self-awareness and sometimes, self-loathing. A time of desperation to fit in and belong. A time of adolescent adventure and a longing to find your true self.
Your body and mind seem to be going in different directions, often without your permission and most times, you just want to shut everyone up, shut the world out, shut yourself away in your bedroom and eat chocolate all day, while playing on your Xbox or feasting on your social media feeds..

This is a season to proclaim guidance – good counsel from family, friends or trusted mentors. The teenage journey isn't one to navigate on your own. You may feel alone but there are a few cheerleaders in your corner who know you will make mistakes and will choose to love you through the turbulent testing times of teenagerhood.

Pause & Ponder

Who can you entrust your current teenage trials to?

Proclamations

Write your personal **Guidance** proclamation

Kindness

My school is filled with kindness
Which is more precious than diamonds
In kindness, we can all find the guidance
To bring a smile to those in sadness, even
with our gentle silence

- 27-

In your school, proclaim kindness

School life can be some of the best years of your life, or some of the worst. You have been assured that "sticks and stones may break your bones but words will never hurt you."

What a stack of lies! The truth is that sticks hurt, stones scar and words can break, bruise and burn us.

Before you start at a new school, or while you're in your current school, proclaim kindness over it and into it. Kindness is a soothing balm that can heal most wounds.

Pause & Ponder

How can your kindness impact your school environment this week?

Proclamations

Write your personal **Kindness** proclamation

Vision

I will go after my vision

Like an athlete going for gold

I will not ignore my mission

To craft a life vision

that is powerful and bold!

- 28-

In your work, proclaim vision

Majority of us will spend the bulk of our lives working. So, it is paramount that you're in a work environment where you feel valued, connected and believed in. The importance of having a vision, no matter where you are on the ladder of your career, cannot be understated. A very wise man once said that without vision, people perish.

Vision gives wings to your future aspirations and stops you from feeling stuck and sluggish at work. Make the time to create your vision statement and own it boldly.

Pause & Ponder

Write your vision statement here

Proclamations

Write your personal **Vision** proclamation

Belonging

We are family by chance and family by choice
I will make space for each of us to have a voice
Some of us are quiet while others make a lot of noise
Together, one another we support, lift up and rejoice

- *29* -

In your family, proclaim belonging

When you throw a bunch of odd balls together, you get an odd-shaped bag filled with odd-shaped balls. Most families feel like this – you don't always want to be together, but you make a choice to invest in your unique family dynamic so that it is a place of belonging, unity and harmony.

The glue of belonging is a compelling family connector that gives space for each person to find themselves, show up as themselves and find their place in the family. Whether you're a parent or a child, your individuality, personality and special quirks will brighten the tapestry of your family.

Pause & Ponder

How can you make space for a family member to feel like they belong?

Proclamations

Write your personal **Belonging** proclamation

Authenticity

As we truly embrace each other
And see our differences as a doorway to discover
One another with fresh eyes of wonder
Our marriage relationship will surely get stronger

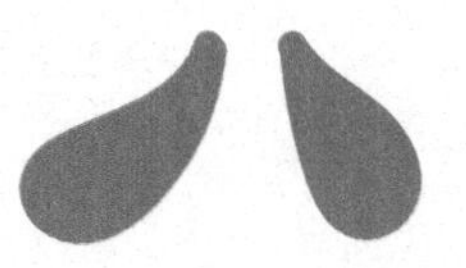

- 30-

In your marriage, proclaim authenticity

The marriage journey is one of twists and turns, magic and mess, growth and groans. You dream of feeling safe, secure and loved unconditionally from the moment you say, "I Do!" Then "life" happens and you begin to hide your true self, cower and compromise, for fear of losing your life partner. This leads to heightened frustration, which can manifest as deep resentment and then lead to the break-up of this most precious relationship.

You were so desperate to protect yourself that you chose not to be your authentic self and eventually your marriage has become an awkward dance of two strangers. Being authentic is paramount to the health of your relationship, so take off your mask and begin to nourish your marriage with all of who you are, right where you are.

Pause & Ponder

Are you being your true self? If not, why not?

Proclamations

Write your personal **Authenticity** proclamation

Loyalty

Parenting is a wonderful gift
My loyalty to my children will never shift
And though I often feel helpless in the mist
I will always lean into loyalty when there's a rift

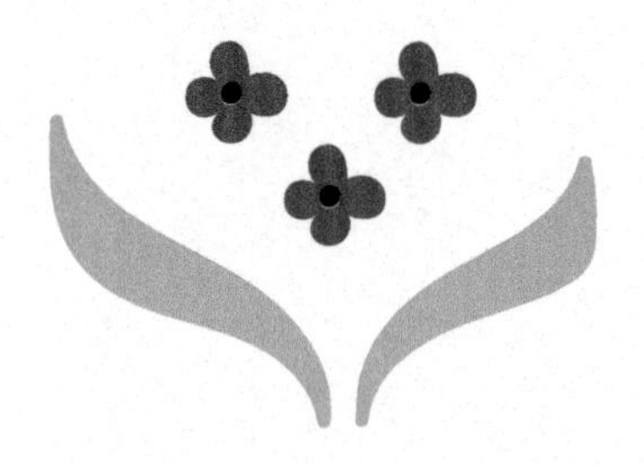

- 31-

In your parenting, proclaim loyalty

Parenting is a word that fills your heart with wonder, excitement and gratitude; along with fear, anxiety and magnitude. As common as parenting is, feeling alone comes naturally. You hide away, thinking your peculiar situation is the most disastrous and dire. You convince yourself that no other family could be as dysfunctional as yours. Parenting in community is a great way to dispel this myth. Trust me, there is nothing new under the sun.

As your children grow up, one of the most important things they need to know is that you have their back, which tells them that you will never leave them or turn your back on them. Loyalty to your children, through the thick and thin of life, pays an abundance of love into their emotional bank accounts – love they can draw on, grow on and invest in others. It is the gift that keeps on giving.

Pause & Ponder

What do you love most about being a parent?

Proclamations

Write your personal **Loyalty** proclamation

Conclusion

So, there you have it.
31 days of poetic proclamations.
31 ways to sow, grow and flow goodness into your life
31 ways for you to create a better world with the power of your words.

Other poems by Peju Abuchi
to give you strength on life's curvy journey

Show up as You

Show up as You
Step out o' the blue
And show up as you
"You" as "you" is a beautiful view!

Show up as you
Take the cue
And show up as you
Out of the multitude
Shine with the few!

Show up as you
Leave nothing behind
And take the front pew
As you show up, you'll light up
Your glow will be true!

Show up as you
It's not as hard as Kung -fu
Saunter onto your stage
And begin to write history on your page

Turn your wounds into wisdom...

Let your wounds teach you
Don't let them tease you

Let your wounds fuel you
Don't let them seal you

Let your wounds raise you
Don't let them phrase you

Let your wounds free you
In all ways to be YOU

Don't let them kill
In them find a thrill -
Not a chill
That pushes others away
But embrace the hope of a brighter day

Allow yourself to say
Without an ounce of grey
That your wounds won't win you over to sin
Instead, you'll use them to turn your world lush and green.

About the Author

Peju "The Spark" Abuchi is a poetic speaker, performance poet, therapeutic wordsmith, and a gifted communicator who believes in the power of curiosity to connect humans and communities. By design, a poet is a healer, thus her passion is centred on bringing hope and healing to a hurting world, through her words.

The hearts of young and old alike have been captivated by Peju's emotive prose and mesmerising poems. This is her "secret sauce" - a unique blend of energy, elocution and effervescence.

An Educator of more than 20 years, she draws on her Masters level qualification in International Studies and Diplomacy to speak to audiences across the globe. She has been featured on BBC Radio, Channels TV, Women in Leadership Publication and The South African Times.

Peju's vision is to influence how people live, love and lead by empowering them with the words to show up, speak up and spark things up – hence her nickname, "The Spark".

She lives in Surrey, UK, with her husband, Obi, and their three exuberant boys.

To hear the author read out the proclamations or to book her, visit *www.pejuabuchi.com*

Printed in Great Britain
by Amazon

37350270R00086